Alaska's

National Parks, Monuments, Preserves and Wildlife Refuges

Distributed by Arctic Circle Enterprises LLC
3812 Spenard Road, Anchorage, AK 99517

Front Cover:
Mt. McKinley, Photo © Hugh Rose/AccentAlaska.com
Exit Glacier, Photo © Ron Niebrugge/AccentAlaska.com
Kennicott Mine, Photo © Dicon Joseph/AccentAlaska.com
Native Totem Pole, Photo © Hugh Rose/AccentAlaska.com

Back Cover:
Photo © Robin Brandt/AccentAlaska.com

© 2007 Designed in USA by Terrell Creative
07G0051 • Printed in China

ISBN-13: 978-1-56944-365-1
ISBN-10: 1-56944-365-3

Contents

Introduction

Alaska is the unspoiled land of superlatives; the highest mountain, longest coastline, largest area, countless lakes, longest days, most glaciers, longest rivers, most wildlife, farthest west, longest winters, fewest roads, longest pipeline, most tundra, shortest summers, fewest humans, and shortest days. This rugged, beautiful, wild land is characterized by its diverse terrain with tall majestic mountains, fjords, bright white landscapes of snow and slow moving, vibrantly colored blue glaciers, dense emerald green forests and bright colorful tundra with wildlife varied and unique to its regions. Sealife abounds, majestic eagles fly freely across its streaming blue skies and giant humpback whales breach from the Pacific's icy waters.

There are 17 national parks in this vast area that protect natural, cultural and historic features of this immense landscape. Alaska, the largest state in the Union, is a state well over twice the size of Texas, able to accommodate our 26 smallest states within its borders, with fewer inhabitants than any of them. Alaska's six distinct regions are: the Arctic, Interior, Southwest, Southcentral, Southeast and the Aleutian region. There are 591,000 square miles to explore with many ways to experience it; wildlife-watching, fishing, hiking, cruises, glacier-viewing, sea kayaking, rafting, snowboarding, and viewing the Northern lights.

Acquired in 1867 from Russia for $7.2 million (about 2 cents an acre), it was admitted to the Union as the 49th state on January 3, 1959, just after World War II. Its rich mineral deposits and large oil reserves have made it one of the most valuable acquisitions in the history of the world.

This beautiful icy land is an American paradise, infusing modern technology with the historic life of old turn-of-the-century mining towns. All are present among the ancient spiritual cultures of the Alaskan natives, evident by their colorful totems, tightly constructed igloos and the mysterious artifacts of Inuit and Aleut people who have lived in this land for over 1,200 years. The art and history of these people have survived and have set the basis for survival in this beautiful harsh land.

Alaska, with its sheer and unsurpassable beauty, is truly one of the most beautiful places in the world.

Chapter One: Arctic

Cape Krusenstern National Monument
Overlook at Cape Krusenstern

© Bob Butterfield/AccentAlaska.com

Noatak National Preserve
Early fall colors of the tundra and Noatak River

Kobuk Valley National Park
Great Kobuk sand dunes 35 miles north of the Arctic Circle

© Tom Walker/AccentAlaska.com

Gates of the Arctic National Park
Arrigetch Peaks at sunset 150 miles north of the Arctic Circle

Arctic National Wildlife Refuge
A Porcupine caribou herd crosses the coastal lagoon.

© Kathy Bushue/AccentAlaska.com

Arctic National Wildlife Refuge
Aurora borealis lights up icebergs on the Beaufort Sea.

Hugh Rose/AccentAlaska.com

Arctic National Wildlife Refuge
Fata Morgana (arctic mirage) hovers over the Beaufort Sea behind a Polar bear in search of food.

Arctic National Wildlife Refuge
Muskoxen on the north slope of the Brooks Range

© Hugh Rose/AccentAlaska.com

Yukon Flats National Wildlife Refuge
Aerial view in winter of oxbow and lakes on the Yukon River. The Canvasback
duck is native to the marshes of Yukon Flats National Wildlife Refuge.

© Matthias Breiter/AccentAlaska.com

Bering Land Bridge National Preserve
Sinuk River

Bering Land Bridge National Preserve
A dog team and musher race across the frozen tundra of Bering Land Bridge National Preserve.

© Paul Souders/AccentAlaska.com

Chapter Two: Interior

Yukon-Charley Rivers National Preserve
Canoe in Yukon River

© Rolf Hicker/AccentAlaska.com

Yukon-Charley Rivers National Preserve
White Birch at Slaven Roadhouse

© Greg Daniels/AccentAlaska.com

Yukon-Charley Rivers National Preserve
Sunset

© Bob Butterfield/AccentAlaska.com

Denali National Park
Mt. McKinley in Alpenglow

Denali National Park
Alaska Range Mountains, Hanging Valley Glaciers

© Bob Butterfield/AccentAlaska.com

Denali National Park
Autumn Wonder Lake

Denali National Park
Aerial view of Mt. McKinley behind Moose's Tooth and Ruth Amphitheater

© Donna Dewhurst/AccentAlaska.com

Denali National Park
Bull caribou and Grizzly Bear

Denali National Park
Moose and Dall Sheep

Chapter Three: Southwest

Becharof National Wildlife Refuge
Red Fox Pup and Brown Bear

Main Photo © William H. Mullins/AccentAlaska.com
Inset Photo © William H. Mullins/AccentAlaska.com

Becharof National Wildlife Refuge
Arctic Forget-Me-Nots and Kejulik Pinnacles

Katmai National Park
Aerial view of Mt. Katmai Caldera that formed after the eruption of 1912

Katmai National Park
Valley of Ten Thousand Smokes and Ukak River

Katmai National Park
Grizzly Bear

© Greg Probst/AccentAlaska.com

Katmai National Park
Bears at Brooks Falls

© Robin Brandt/AccentAlaska.com

Lake Clark National Park
A bush plane pilot fishes near his float plane on Lake Clark.

© Steve Kaufman/AccentAlaska.com

Chapter Four: Southcentral

Kenai Fjords National Park
Aialik Glacier

Kenai Fjords National Park
Exit Glacier

© Ron Niebrugge/AccentAlaska.com

Kenai Fjords National Park
Bear Glacier in Resurrection Bay

© Kim Heacox/AccentAlaska.com

Kenai Fjords National Park
The Harding Ice Field flows into Exit Glacier.

© Ron Niebrugge/AccentAlaska.com

Wrangell-St. Elias National Park
Root Glacier

Wrangell-St. Elias National Park
Kennicott Mine

Wrangell-St. Elias National Park
Kennicott, Gates and Root Glaciers

© John Markel/AccentAlaska.com

Wrangell-St. Elias National Park
Aerial view of Hubbard Glacier and Russell Fjord

Chapter Five: Southeast

Glacier Bay National Park
Aerial view of John Hopkins Inlet in winter

© Sean Neilson/AccentAlaska.com

© Sean Neilson/AccentAlaska.com

Glacier Bay National Park
Seal Herd

© Kim Heacox/AccentAlaska.com

Glacier Bay National Park
Sunrise on the Fairweather Range above the Hugh Miller Inlet

Glacier Bay National Park
A cruise ship sits at the base of Margerie Glacier.

© Hugh Rose/AccentAlaska.com

Misty Fjords National Monument
A flightseeing plane passes over Nooya Lake.

© Steve Gilroy/AccentAlaska.com

Admiralty Island National Monument
An old cannery and boats rest at the entrance to Mitchell Bay near Angoon.

© Kim Heacox/AccentAlaska.com

Sitka National Historic Park
Native Totem Poles

Main Photo © Steve Gilroy/AccentAlaska.com
Inset Photo © Ken Graham/AccentAlaska.com

Klondike Gold Rush National Historic Park
The 33-mile-long Chilkoot Trail was established by
Tlingit people as a trade route into the interior of Canada.

© Ken Garaham/AccentAlaska.com

Klondike Gold Rush National Historic Park
Aerial view of the Port of Skagway, Chilkoot Pass and Dyea

Chapter Six: Aleutian

Aniakchak National Monument and Preserve
Aniakchak Caldera

© Donna Dewhurst/AccentAlaska.com